salute
to a sufferer

LESLIE D. WEATHERHEAD

salute
to a sufferer

an attempt to offer the
plain man a Christian
philosophy of suffering

ABINGDON PRESS ♪ new york nashville

SALUTE TO A SUFFERER

Copyright © 1962 by Leslie D. Weatherhead

Library of Congress Catalog Card Number: 63-8669

MANUFACTURED IN U. S. A.

This book is dedicated to my friends

Norman and Hansie French

as a small token of my appreciation and
gratitude for all that they have done to
make a yoke easy and a burden light

Preface

First of all I must acknowledge the great honor in being invited to deliver one of the Peake Memorial Lectures. My predecessors in this lectureship have all been scholars. I have no claim whatever to be a scholar. I have been a working minister ever since I was ordained. In this capacity I have tried to bring the truths which scholarship uncovers and by which men live, and set them in simple language before needy men and women.

This I think would appeal to Dr. Peake. A great scholar, a devout saint, and a great student and lover of the Bible, he was nevertheless a modern in the best sense of the word. He was far too eager-minded to be imprisoned in theories of verbal inspiration and dead formulas. For him revelation was progressive both within the Bible and after its completion. Truth is unchanging, but man's appreciation of truth widens with his increasing insight and understanding, and man must be free to break out of every verbal prison, however venerable and sacred, when the light of the Holy Spirit, pledged to guide us into all truth, shines upon him. He who is unwilling to move cannot be guided anywhere.

I hope nothing in this book will upset the reader. I think there is nothing contrary to the teaching of Christ and its implications, and therefore I think that Dr. Peake, whom I came so deeply to admire and love, would not disapprove.

What I have tried to do is to imagine that I am writing this book for a Christian friend of ordinary education and outlook

7

who has suddenly fallen seriously ill, perhaps incurably ill, o whose wife or child has done so.

I imagine that his mind is in a whirl of confusion about it. He has never given much thought to the problems inherent in the mystery of suffering. How can his mind find peace? He knows there are many questions which no one can answer. But is there a philosophy of suffering which can give to his troubled mind a place where it can find rest? How can he fit this terrible verdict of his doctors into the teaching he has accepted throughout the whole of his Christian life—that God is both utterly good and all-powerful? Why should this event befall *him*? Is it the will of God to be placidly accepted? Is it fate? Is is accident? Is it bad luck? Is it a punishment for some sin of long ago? Should he rely on doctors or should he seek help from so-called faith healers? Should he ask his fellow Christians to pray for him, and if so, what should he expect to happen? Are prayer and faith likely to succeed where medicine fails? What should be his mental attitude if all that he can do fails to avert death?

These, in my experience, are the questions men ask when suffering of body or mind—either their own or that of a dear one—descends upon them. I have no glib, easy, final answers. The element of mystery remains. The demand on faith remains. Trying to answer mental problems does little to make pain easier to bear. If all were explained, suffering remains to be faced and borne, and intellectual answers do not supply courage and faith. These are of far greater importance and far greater value than understanding. I can only hope to banish a few false ideas which make the problem darker than it need be and with which many sufferers mentally torture themselves.

Let us then go into this dim cathedral called human pain. It is a sacred place. Many who have served the world best have suffered most. Many, with even less light than we have, have been quite unbroken by their suffering. Their faith has triumphed. There are many windows in the cathedral, so that we do not walk in black darkness. And under the eastern window, beyond which the sun of understanding rises ever higher in the sky, is a cross which whispers its eternal message that God himself in Christ came right down into our pain and shared it. He understands how we feel. He promises that one day we shall understand too.

In 1755 when John Wesley wrote his famous *Notes on the New Testament,* he said in the Preface:

I write chiefly for plain, unlettered men who understand only their mother-tongue and love the Word of God and have a desire to save their souls. . . . I have used all such methods of reasoning and modes of expression as people in common life are acquainted with.

It is also recorded that when he had completed the writing of a sermon he would frequently read it over to the kitchen maid so as to discover any word or phrase that was beyond her understanding. If he did discover one he would substitute a simpler. I have long had the ambition to speak and write so that anyone of fifteen years and upwards could understand.

So, in ten brief chapters, written as simply as I can, I have tried to shed on this dark mystery a tiny bit of light which I have gathered during my forty-five years' ministry. The chapter headings indicate the line of argument followed.

I feel that I must express my gratitude to my wife, who always takes such a helpful interest in anything I write and has once more helped me to correct the proofs, and to my friend, Miss Elsie B. Thompson, who has given me invaluable help in preparing this little book for the press.

—LESLIE D. WEATHERHEAD

Contents

Chapter 1

Does God want me to be ill?

MY ANSWER TO THAT IS AN EMPHATIC NO! MY EVIDENCE IS the nature of God as Jesus revealed him. Jesus kept on telling men that one of the best clues to the nature of God they could find anywhere is the nature of man at his best. He said to them, "If ye then, being evil"—or grudging, as I am told the Greek word means—"know how to give good gifts unto your children, how much more shall your Father which is in heaven give good things to them that ask him?" (Matt. 7:11 K.J.V.) Truly, as every father knows, there are some gifts a father must not give at all, and others which he must not give until certain conditions are fulfilled, and others again, the gift of which would express favoritism. But who has met a father who did not want all his sons and daughters to have good health?

The temporary pain that warns that something is wrong is a good thing, and a father would desire it. The cut finger and the burned hand warn the child, and we hardly need so eminent an authority as Sir Russell Brain to tell us that "insensitivity to pain can be far more dangerous than the actual suffering of it." [1] But chronic, long-continued pain and disease cannot represent the will of God in any intelligent use of the word "will."

God's ideal intention for all his sons and daughters is perfect health of body, mind, and spirit. The whole healing ministry of Jesus proves, both by deed and word, that this is so. When

[1] Sir Russell Brain, now Lord Brain, past president of the Royal College of Physicians, lecturing on "Pain" to the annual professional nurses' and midwives' conference in London. (*The Times* [London], October 17, 1961.)

a poor woman who had been ill for eighteen years was brought to Jesus, he healed her. So far from leaving her ill and telling her that her illness was the "will of God," he referred to her in no uncertain way as "this woman whom *Satan* hath bound . . . these eighteen years" (Luke 13:16 K.J.V.).[2] Whether we regard "Satan" as a powerful evil intelligence or as a useful "type-name" for the evil that befalls us from the mass ignorance, folly, and sin of mankind, does not affect the question. Any pain worth calling "suffering" is evil. It is something that ought not to be. It is something we must endlessly labor to remove. Let us never look upon some human form, stricken with disease, and say, "This is the will of God." On the morning when all the newspapers announce that yet another disease is conquered and banished let us then say, "Thy will be done."

God may be thought of not only as Father but as the great Artist, an artist who has not yet completed his work but still labors at his task. As Jesus said, "My Father *has never yet ceased his work,* and I am working too." (John 5:17 N.E.B.)[3] God is hindered in that ceaseless task because he has chosen, in so many situations, to work in co-operation with man. When he makes a sunset he does it alone, but when he makes human health he puts up with man's interference, is hindered by man's ignorance, folly and sin, and waits for man's co-operation. But this does not alter his *desire,* or deny that his *will* is perfect health. What artist would *desire* or *will* any imperfection in any part of his creation? What musician, poet, or sculptor would *desire* a flaw anywhere in his work?

Further, it is when we have perfect health at every point of our being that we can offer to God a maximum usefulness. In

[2] Italics mine.
[3] Italics mine.

this study we shall look at the Cross again and again and see what Christ attained through his suffering and what we can still attain through ours, but as he moved through Galilee, Jesus would have been of *less* use to God if he had been lame, or blind, or crippled, or diabetic, or rheumatic.

No one denies that immense good has been achieved in the world by the suffering saints, but it was not the suffering that made them saints. It was their reaction to suffering. It was such a splendid reaction that they accomplished far more good than most people accomplish with their health. The suffering awakened them spiritually and they reacted nobly. But *if they had been equally awakened* without the challenge of illness and pain, as their Master was, they could have been of even more use to him because they could have offered him in their bodies a *perfect* instrument for his will. God does not *need* any kind of evil—and suffering is evil—to accomplish his good, although he endlessly seeks to bring his good out of man's evil.

The notion that pain, in itself, makes people saintly should be put to a relentless test by the one who asserts this error. Next time he has a severe toothache, or drops a heavy stone on his foot, he should tell himself that he is at once nobler for the pain involved, and we should make sure to ask those who live with him whether they agree with him!

I find it hard to understand how anyone who loves and thinks can contemplate a human being racked with pain and say in his heart, "This is the will of God," "This is what God wanted to happen." Think of a lovely teen-age girl reveling in life, delighting, as she should, in the health of her body which allows her to swim, to dance, to play tennis, to climb the hills, suddenly stricken down with poliomyelitis, lying with twisted limbs and paralyzed back, with all her dreams of career or marriage and

15

motherhood broken. If it is the *will* of anyone that this should happen, he must be a fiend from hell; and to say, "This is the will of God," when Jesus said it was Satan, seems to me a far worse blasphemy than any other theological denial could be.

Let us not label as "the will of God" a situation for which, if he could accomplish it, a man would be lodged in a criminal lunatic asylum or sent for a long period to jail.

I am hoping in this book to bring comfort to people who are ill, and the very first thing I want to say to them is that God does not want them to be ill. He wants them to be well. He must not do for his human family what it must learn to do for itself. He must not, as it were, do our homework for us, or have individual favorites, but he is not just sympathizing with the individual sufferer. He is sharing the suffering.

Further, God is ever fighting, in all the ways that perfect love and holiness and power make justifiable, to get his will done; that is, to make us perfectly well in body, mind, and spirit.

God can be *temporarily* defeated—and we shall study this point —for if he were not, man's freedom would be a farce. Even if we do not recover in the way we wish, God is not finally defeated, as we shall see. In the meantime, let us hold on to the thought that so far from being God's will, our suffering is something he is actively trying to overcome. God is actively at work, outside us, in the activities of those who are treating us, and within us, seeking to remove everything which delays recovery and to quicken everything that speeds it.

Chapter 2

But surely it is God who allows my suffering?

THE ANSWER TO THAT QUESTION MUST BE, "YES, HE DOES." LET US clear our minds at once by the thought that, like a human parent, God allows what he does not will. He *allows* human sin, or man would have no real free will. He does not will or intend sin. God is responsible for its possibility, not for its actuality.

If your little boy is learning to walk in the living room where there is a soft carpet, you *allow* him to stumble and even fall. You don't *intend* him to fall or you would push him over. And you make sure of the conditions in which he is learning. The living room is all right, where there's a thick carpet, but a busy intersection is not, nor is a room where he could do himself lasting harm; where there could arise a situation which would do more harm than good; where your purpose would be defeated.

So, in the case of suffering, which so often comes to the individual through the ignorance or folly or sin of the human family to which a man belongs rather than through any fault of his own, God *allows* the suffering because he wants the human family to learn, to substitute knowledge for its ignorance, wisdom for its folly, and holiness for its sin; and these three exchanges cannot be imposed on human nature. They have to be achieved by the hard way of learning.

But God would not *allow* a situation to befall us which would defeat his purpose ultimately, any more than you would with your child. So the very fact that he *allows* it to happen has a

17

hidden treasure for us which is worth picking up. If he *allows* it, it means he can use it for our good. So far from its defeating his purpose, he can use it as you use a fall to teach your child to walk. If this is true, the measure of any present calamity must be the measure of our faith, since both are less than the measure of his loving purposefulness and desire to use the evil he did not will.

Let us turn to the best illustration of all, the cross of Christ. It must be stated fearlessly that the cross was not the will of God in the sense of being God's intention. Jesus did not come into the world to be murdered. He came to be followed. Any opposite view involves the deduction that Judas, Pilate, and the evil, crafty priests were pawns in a divine game and carrying out a divine plan. This is impossible logic. It was wicked men who put Christ to death. Peter stated this clearly on the occasion of his very first sermon. He spoke of Jesus and said, "[Whom] you crucified and killed by the hands of lawless men." (Acts 2:23.)[1] Wicked men do not do the will of God; they do the opposite.

When Jesus was in the garden of Gethsemane he could easily have run away. The disciples did. But he was in a dilemma. He must either run away or be crucified. *In those circumstances imposed on him by evil men,* we can say that it was God's will that he should be crucified, and so we hear him say, "Nevertheless, not as I will, but as thou wilt," but it was only what I have called in another book, God's circumstantial will.[2] It is incredible that God's ideal intention was that his dear Son should be murdered and that men should commit sin to do God's will.

So, if you like, you can say of your illness, that *in the circum-*

[1] God's foreknowledge we shall look at later.
[2] See *The Will of God* (Nashville: Abingdon Press, 1944).

stances of evil imposed on the human family by ignorance, folly, or sin, it is God's will that you should be ill rather than be a favorite, magically immune or delivered from what others have to face. But do keep the thought clearly in mind that God's ideal intention, what he *wants,* is health.

Similarly, a man might want his son to be an architect. This might be his ideal intention and he might help the boy to train for this profession, but if war came, then *in the circumstances imposed on the community by the evil called war,* the father might want his son to do his bit in the army, navy, or air force. But how wrong it would be to suppose that fighting was the father's will for his boy. Architecture was the father's will.

But the story of the Cross takes us further and is very relevant to the whole problem of suffering. Christ did not just passively endure it while God looked on. He took such an attitude to it, accepting it in such a positive and trusting spirit, that he wrested from it triumph and victory. He did not just meet the evil that men did to him as one might meet the debit account in a ledger with a credit amount that canceled it out. He used the evil. He turned the debit into a credit, so that Good Friday is not a sad story with a happy ending on Easter Day. Both are days of triumph as we look back on them.

Good Friday was terrible for Jesus beyond our power to compute. The Cross felt like defeat. It looked like defeat. It was called defeat. It seemed as if evil had triumphed and his cause was lost. He felt deserted even by his Father. But that suffering love which would not run away revealed itself to be the greatest redemptive force the world has ever known. As H. H. Farmer once pointed out, "You cannot defeat defeat." Men could only "look on him whom they had pierced" and break down at the wonder and grandeur and power of such a revelation of the nature of God.[3]

Present illness can be very depressing. We too can feel lonely and even deserted by God. I know that when I was ill in a hospital for many weeks some years ago, I felt very lonely, perplexed, and miserable. But suffering can be what businessmen call a "frozen asset." We cannot realize on it yet, and while suffering continues we may be unable to see anything remotely like an asset about it; but gradually, especially as we look back on it, we can take such an attitude to it that we can do what Jesus did: offer it to God and in so doing help him turn it into a victory for our own souls and of use to others whom he is trying to help.

To me one of the most wonderful truths in religion is that God can use evil in his overall plan as powerfully as he can use good; not indeed for our happiness but for our final well-being and the establishment of his kingdom. This, of course, does not enable us to say that if evil is done "it doesn't much matter because God will use it." Evil costs crucifixion. It hurts God and often man, and is always a temporary hindrance.

But the whole meaning of omnipotence is not that everything that happens is God's will. Clearly, in a world where there is free will, where men learn slowly and make mistakes, where men act foolishly, blindly, uncomprehendingly, and sometimes sinfully; in a world where we are so closely bound together that we make one another suffer—in such a world a million things can happen which are not the will of God. Many are the opposite. Omnipotence means that nothing that is allowed to happen has within itself the power finally and ultimately to defeat God.

[3] I have tried to work out the meaning of the Cross for us today in a book entitled, *A Plain Man Looks at the Cross* (Nashville: Abingdon Press, 1945).

As the psalmist said in a moment of amazing insight, "Surely the wrath of men shall praise thee." (Ps. 76:10.)

Not *in spite of* the Cross but *through* the Cross, the ultimate aim of God in Christ was achieved as completely as it would have been had men followed Christ from the first instead of murdering him. That is why we place the Cross in the very center of what we call God's plan of redemption.

So, in the case of human suffering, God does not will it or desire it, but finally it will not defeat him in his plan for the individual sufferer—and he has such a plan for each one of us. The fact that the suffering is allowed at all carries the guarantee that God, so far from being defeated by it finally, can weave it into a pattern as wonderful as one which left it out. God can bring us, not in spite of our suffering, but because of it and his use of it, and our reaction to it, to the same place as we should have reached if suffering had never come our way and with final gain instead of loss.

Indeed, I feel that the teaching of the Bible is that suffering is an asset almost to be coveted. After all, our heroes are not those for whom life has always been prosperous and painless. We all want to be healthy, happy, and to possess enough money to allow life to run smoothly and easily. Yet the pulpit illustrations held up before us are rarely drawn from such people. Now that I am at the receiving end of sermons I notice how all the illustrations —and my own were the same—are drawn from the lives of those who suffered in body, mind, estate, or in their planning, and who yet turned loss into asset and dross into gold. Without desiring to suffer we all agree that "the mark of rank in nature is capacity for pain," and certainly suffering which is gladly undertaken for the sake of others can hardly be listed as evil at all,

21

since it ennobles the one who bears it, the one who benefits by it, and all who see it or hear of it.

Commenting on the idea of suffering, Harry Emerson Fosdick puts the matter well.[4]

Far from being an occasion of shame, in the writer's eyes, the church's sufferings [i.e., the sufferings of church members endured] were a cause of hope, since their explanation lay not behind in past sin but ahead in future good consequence—"All chastening seemeth for the present to be not joyous but grievous; yet afterward it yieldeth peaceable fruit. . . ." This conviction that an untroubled life is uneducated, that to deal with tragedy is to handle reality and to deal well with it is a great gain, that no softly cushioned life can ever be wise or strong or good, runs throughout the Testament. Not sporadic and occasional, but constant and fundamental is this treatment of affliction as opportunity, not disgrace, an indispensable implement for building faith and character, rather than a means for their destruction.

In the light of all this, two sayings may well be true. First, that what happens to us eventually matters little, but our reaction to what happens to us matters much. Second, a French saying which roughly translated runs, "To suffer passes. To have suffered, never passes." The pain of body and mind will cease one day. But what we learn in these dark experiences is our treasure forever. It is a treasure no one can take from us.

[4] *A Guide to Understanding the Bible* (New York: Harper & Row, 1938), p. 185. Italics mine.

Chapter 3

Didn't God know that suffering would fall upon me?

THE ANSWER AGAIN IS "YES." BUT LET US LOOK AT WHAT LIES behind the question. Probably there are two doubts in the sufferer's mind. He might well say to me, "You say that most suffering falls on men from the world's (if not the individual's) ignorance, folly, and sin. But God *knew* from the beginning that men would be ignorant, foolish, and sinful. He made them that way. So, if those three things bring suffering, he willed that suffering. Secondly, if he *knew* it would happen, it *had* to happen."

Let us look at the second point first. The fact that God knows beforehand what is going to happen does not make it happen. If I go to the door beyond which is a starving dog, and if I open it and hold out a lovely, meaty bone, I *know* that the dog will move toward the bone. But it is not my knowing that makes the dog move. It is his hunger. I *know* that after a service in church the bulk of the congregation will get up and walk out, but it is not my knowing that moves them.

The truth probably is that the future stands to God in the same relation as the past does. Men speak of "an eternal present" to cover past, present, and future. Now even we, who know the past, do not look back and say, "It was my present knowing of the past that made past events happen." The truth is that the events determined the knowledge. Why then should we suppose that a *present* knowing of the future makes future events happen?

23

It is not God's foreknowledge of events that makes them happen. It is their happening—and he can see the future as we see the past—that determines his knowledge. In regard to our illnesses he knows all the long chain of events that leads up to illness, but it is not his knowing that is the determining factor.

The first part of the doubt in the questioner's mind must be answered honestly. God must have known and decreed that men should learn slowly and have freedom to be foolish and to commit sin. That is why in the last chapter I emphasized the difference between what God wills and what God allows.

He *allows* ignorance and folly and sin. Can we imagine a world in which men were magically supplied with all the knowledge they would need to avoid suffering, all the wisdom they would need to have had magically implanted so that no foolish act would ever be committed? And what would holiness be if it were mechanical, if man were not *free* to sin? God himself cannot take two naturally contradictory paths of action at the same time. He cannot endow "holiness" with any value and at the same time make impossible man's freedom to sin.

We must admit then that God is responsible for the possibility, nay the probability, of suffering, but he ever seeks to implant the opposite of its causes, that is, knowledge instead of ignorance, wisdom instead of folly, and holiness instead of sin. Further, he knows that where those opposites cannot be established he can still make evil serve his purposes, and this is the justification of its possibility.

The Bible often speaks of suffering as fire, and the very use of the word is a compliment to human nature. It implies gold. "Wood, hay, and stubble" are *destroyed* by fire. Gold is purified by it. If our reaction is right, God can use the suffering that falls upon us from the ignorance, folly, and sin in the world—our own and other people's—as fire is used upon gold. Unbearable and intolerable as we often feel suffering to be, it is a sign that God cares enough to bother with us. Wouldn't it be much easier if he either blotted us out altogether or was content to use his power merely to achieve our happiness instead of bothering with our characters? The refiner of gold goes on using fire until he can see his own image reflected in the gold. God seems to do the same with men, using the fire *he* did not make to serve his purposes (I Cor. 3:12-15; I Pet. 1:7).

C. S. Lewis made much of this point in his book *The Problem of Pain,*[1] and I am indebted to him here. Think of the number of people who are fond of dogs. A trained dog who is a household pet lives longer, is far happier, and is more highly cultured —one might say, is nicer to know—than the wild, untrained animal of the prairie or the pariah dog that haunts an Eastern city. A man who loves his dog washes it when it doesn't want to be washed. He housebreaks it, refusing to allow it to befoul his house. He may strike it to stop it from stealing. It is a matter of great importance to the man that the dog should not be repulsive in its habits. He takes infinite pains with it. Why? Because through discipline there is more than a chance that the man can bring the dog into a communion with himself higher and deeper than would otherwise be possible. If the dog could think and talk to other dogs, no doubt the experience he underwent at the hands of the man would lead him to confide to other dogs that his master could not possibly love him since he suffered so much. His doggy dignity would often be lowered and his happiness temporarily destroyed. But the sufferings of the dog and the trouble of the man are a compliment to the dog. After

[1] (New York: The Macmillan Company, 1944.)

25

all, a man does not go to the same trouble with a rat or a frog. Presumably they are incapable of being brought into such a high communion with man.

Look at the relationship between God and man in a similar way, save that *God uses a whip already provided by the effects of man's ignorance, folly, and sin,* whereas the man in relation to the dog introduces the whip from outside the situation. But God uses the whip of human suffering for the same purpose—namely, to bring man into communion with him.

We may see the thought of the compliment in a different illustration. A child brings his autograph album to a great composer who, to please the child, scribbles a few bars in the book and the child is contented about it. But look at the trouble that composer takes with his great masterpiece, writing, rubbing out, rewriting, introducing this harmony, varying that melody, as Beethoven did with his sonatas. It doesn't require a wild flight to try to imagine that the composition is itself sentient. It might complain and say: "I wish he would not keep rubbing me out and re-writing. I was all right as I was." We know that the truth is that the pains the composer takes are a compliment to the composition. It is just because it is a masterpiece that it merits so much more care than the hastily scribbled bars which please the child.

We could find another illustration in the attitude of the great poet to his poem. Those who have seen the original of Tennyson's *In Memoriam* say that he hardly left a line unaltered. He wrote it, then scratched it out, and then altered the arrangement of the verses, when one might imagine the poem saying, "My lines rhymed before. Why can't he let me alone?" But to be left alone would mean that the poet was content with something less than the best, less than something that the poem might become.

Herein is illustrated in part our attitude to God.[2] When trouble assails us we cry out to God and say, "We wish you would leave us alone. All we want is to be happy." But the trouble the Artist takes to use every kind of discipline that evil brings into life as a means of purifying our character, though intolerable to us at the time, is a tremendous compliment; and when we cry out to be left alone we are asking for less care, not more care; for less love, not more love. We are like a dog, unwashed, filthy, and with stinking habits, saying, "I only want to be left alone." But the God who left us alone as we are now would not be God. Therefore God will use any means, including the suffering he does not will, to shape us and alter us and improve us and win us from our wild, filthy, foul, and unclean habits, so that at last we may be made ready to enter into a communion with him, the depths of which have never been plumbed.

Let me lighten our thought by recalling a Sunday-school treat to which with great delight I went as a child. We had a benevolent superintendent who greatly desired that we should all have a happy day. Those who ran in the races and won got a prize, but those who came in last got a surreptitious sweet. At the end of the day "a good time had been had by all." But the attitude of the superintendent was kindness rather than love. Love has in it a stern note, something stronger than mere benevolence. Kindness makes us happy, but it has no power in it to make us improve. Love has.

In the City Temple we have what is called an adoption scheme. Poor and underprivileged families are adopted by individuals or groups of individuals, and Miss Jones from the City Temple goes

---

[2] I say "in part" because in the above illustrations the imperfection is the fault of the composer and poet. In our relationship to God, the fault of imperfection lies with us.

to visit her adopted family and showers pennies and sweets on the children. She doesn't bother much if they are filthy or foul-mouthed or have runny noses. But their *mother* is much more concerned about these things because she loves them with a love that is greater than mere benevolence and kindness. We cannot imagine a true father saying about his son: "I don't care if he is filthy and a liar and a knave and a cheat so long as he is happy." Happiness is not a true end. It is always a by-product. Character is the end, for our character development contributes to the glory of God which is the end of all human existence.

Now look from these illustrations at God's relationship with us. We ask him to be kind. There is a true sense in which God is not kind. His relationship with us is bigger and grander and closer. Kindness is often a love substitute which we offer to people whom we may not love, cannot love, or cannot be bothered to love, and kindness is too poor a thing to express God's relationship to us. We keep on pleading with him to be kind because we want to be happy. His attitude is higher and deeper. He *loves* us because he wants to bring us into communion with him and he knows that we cannot be really deeply, completely, and permanently happy until we have been brought into communion with him. Whereas if he is merely kind, we shall make happiness our goal and be content with something less than the best, with something less than we may yet become, something less than God can make us, and when we ask God to be kind to us that we may be happy, we are asking for less love, not more; we are being content to remain wild dogs, we are being content to be the rapidly scribbled half-dozen bars of music instead of the master-piece, we are being content to be the rhyme instead of the poem.

When I think about God I realize that, in weak moments of self-indulgence, I should like to live in a world where "a good time was had by all," where God was kind and everybody was happy. But in better moments I realize that it would be asking for a love substitute, kindness. It would be being content with happiness instead of character. If we could see deeper into the nature of reality, including the things that are unseen, we should realize that the things we want which are not his will, ultimately bring only more suffering and misery however innocent they seem, however badly we want them, however passionately we insist on having them, however accompanied they may be by brilliant planning, and however marked they may be by what the world calls success. Our truest happiness is a by-product of our quest for blessedness, and blessedness is the complete identity of our will with God's and the fullest realization of our communion with him.

Paul puts it like this: "Our light affliction, which is but for a moment, worketh for us a far more exceeding and eternal weight of glory; while we look not at the things which are seen, but at the things which are not seen: for the things which are seen are temporal; but the things which are not seen are eternal." (II Cor. 4: 17-18 K.J.V.) There is possible to us the glory of sons caught up into the Father's fellowship, honored by the Father's love, brought into communion by his endless patience and the suffering which both he and we endure. This thought can stay us in the hour of our anguish and nerve us in the day of our distress. I only have to look into my own heart to be certain of this: that if God were content with me as I am, it could only mean that he had stopped caring and had given me up as a bad job.

Chapter 4

Why should this happen to me?

THIS IS THE VERY NATURAL QUESTION WITH WHICH WE ALL lash ourselves when our own suffering or that of a dear one comes to upset our lives. A woman who wrote to me when her husband died, leaving her with three little children, allows me to quote from her letter: "I have tortured myself thinking of all the human failings I have had in the past in our lives together and how I could have been a much better wife. I keep telling myself that I must have done something *awful* to deserve this."

All through my ministry the same problem has pressed upon my mind. In one's church it sometimes seemed as if the most valuable members were stricken down. Some others, from whose nagging and criticism one would have enjoyed a brief holiday, boasted about the truth that they had "never had a day's illness." Why does suffering come to one who certainly does not deserve it and pass by another who, in our judgment, does?

Let us honestly try to think out a Christian answer to the question, "Why should this happen to me?" remembering two preliminary ideas. (1) Many non-Christians in Eastern lands have their answer ready and it is mentally satisfying to them. They say that we have lived before in an earlier incarnation and that the cause of present suffering runs back into earlier lives, and the effect of our life now, including our reaction to present pain, will be harvested in future lives. I do not find this answer convincing, though I do not feel that there is anything contrary to Christ's teaching in it. Indeed, there is evidence that it was held to be orthodox in the Christian church for the first few centuries and that, although never of vital importance, it was part of the mental background of the Gospels.[1] We read, for instance, that the disciples asked Jesus about one man, "Rabbi, who sinned, this man or his parents, that he was born blind?" (John 9:2.) Clearly, if the patient's own sin had brought blindness from *birth,* the sin must have been committed in an earlier life. Jesus did not rebuke this as if it were erroneous thinking. His reply was significant, and to get its truth we must rearrange the punctuation which in Greek is absent altogether. Jesus' answer should not be misunderstood to mean that the man was born blind in order that he might provide an occasion for Christ to show his miraculous power. The passage should read: "It was not that this man sinned, or his parents." (Note the full stop.) "But that the works of God might be made manifest in him we must work the works of him who sent me, while it is day." Christ seemed unready to theorize about why the man was blind, save to deny that sin had caused his blindness. He seemed eager first to make the patient see. That was the priority in the situation.

A second preliminary thought we should honestly hold in mind is that we only ask, "Why should this happen to me?" when *trouble* befalls us. When some lovely girl consents to become our wife, when a perfect baby is born into our home, or when we are given some coveted position in our trade or profession, we rarely ask, "Why should this happen to me?"

The truth is that only rarely can we put our finger on the cause of our suffering. One's own folly, ignorance, or sin *may* have brought one's troubles on oneself. In these days we realize that faulty emotions long harbored deep in the mind can touch

[1] I have worked out this idea in a pamphlet called, *The Case for Reincarnation,* obtainable from Mrs. Peto, 16 Kingswood Rd., Tadworth, Surrey, England, or from the City Temple, London, E.C.1.

off, or even cause, disease and nervous breakdown. Such emotions as worry, terror, and prolonged anxiety appear to be able to set off troubles like gastric or duodenal ulcers and asthma; while resentment, bitterness, and jealousy sometimes appear to lie behind some forms of arthritis. Repressed hatred seems even to lead to outbursts resembling epilepsy, and guilt is suspected to be behind some forms of skin and digestive troubles. But it is very dangerous to suppose that this is *always* so, and often such a conclusion is quite inaccurate, and also unfair and unkind.

It is healthy enough that we should examine ourselves about this; but more frequently no causal connection can be established, and it is morbid continually to lash one's memory by endlessly asking, "Why did this happen to me?"

The truth is that in regard to human suffering we are all in it together. No one, even if he could prove that a particular experience of suffering was *not* his own fault, could really feel exonerated from *a* contribution to the total of human suffering. In his fine book *A Doctor's Casebook in the Light of the Bible,* Dr. Paul Tournier truly says:

> I realized that it is absolutely impossible by intellectual processes to separate that of which we are the victims from that for which we are to blame. . . . The Cross is at one and the same time forgiveness where we are guilty, and true relief where we are the victims.[2]

In many ways it seems to me that life is like a game of hockey. In the clash of bodies driven by opposing wills, someone is going to get hurt. If we are playing we might ask, "Why *not* me?" In such a game the goalkeeper may never have to save a shot. In another game he may get a dislocated shoulder. But he does not

[2] (New York: Harper & Row, 1960.)

say either about immunity or accident, "Why did this happen to me?" He is a member of the team and is more concerned with whether his side wins or loses. He says, *"We* lost," or, *"We* won," and if you ask him about the shoulder he will say, "Oh! that's just one of those things—the breaks of the game." He knows that in a game like hockey one must take the risk of personal injury, and he doesn't think of it as personal. It's all in the game.

I think in the game of life, in which there is such a clash of purposes and wills, in which we are all very ignorant, in which we all make mistakes and do foolish and sinful things, and in which we are so bound up together that what I do and know and say affects other lives, someone is bound to get hurt without there being any answer to the question, "Why should this happen to *me?"* save to say that you were in the team. Your disaster is your share of the team's adventure. Often it is the thrill of health and happiness. Sometimes it is the burden of ill health and unhappiness. But the Christian believes that in the game of life the *team* will win and he finds a measure of comfort in that fact. The Captain has assured him that the team cannot lose. Thomas Carlyle has a word for the individual sufferer here: "For us was thy back bent, for us were thy straight limbs and fingers so deformed; thou wert our conscript on whom the lot fell, and fighting our battles wast so marred."

So part of the answer to the question at the beginning of this chapter must be, "Because you belong to the human family." Your suffering is part of the price the team pays in its great struggle toward perfection. We will cope later with the retort, "But that is unfair to me."

This matter of the suffering that comes to us because we belong to the human family is important enough to demand further explanation.

Even God could not arrange human life on two bases which are mutually contradictory *or give men the benefits which derive from both*. Two possibilities lay before him. He could arrange life on the individual basis or on the family basis. He chose to arrange life on the family basis, and by "family" I mean the great human family.

We can see how wise this basis is if we imagine life arranged on the basis of the individual instead of the family. Had God chosen the former method, then nothing would have come to us through the misdeeds or ignorance or folly of others, but, also, nothing would have come to us through the wisdom, courage, and nobility of others. We should not have to carry the burden of others; but neither should we ever be carried by the wings of others. Nothing undeserved, whether an asset or a liability, would ever have come to us. We should live an individual life. The innocent would never suffer.

To sit down and let the mind imaginatively conceive an existence where everything was cut off from us that did not come to us through our own merit, is to feel a tremendous relief that the government of the world is in the hands of a God who saw far enough ahead to plan the world on the family basis and save us from the curse of individualism. Take one example. Suppose you fell ill through your own fault. No wisdom could be at your disposal save your own; no kindly sympathy or nursing; no knowledge in other men's brains; no skill in other men's fingers. What happens today? You are whirled to a hospital in a car which, in itself, represents the brains of a thousand men through a long period of years. At the hospital you are tended by the patient skill and nursing of others. Inventions and discoveries of brilliant men of all nations and all ages are at your disposal through the training the doctor has had. In a word, the brains and the skill of the

34

family are at your beck and call. As an individualist you would have died like a dog in a ditch.

Nor is it only in emergency that we gain from belonging to the family. As has often been said, "When I rise and go to my bath a cake of soap is handed me by a Frenchman, a sponge is handed me by a Pacific Islander, a towel by a Turk, my underclothes by one Englishman, my outer garments by another. I come down to breakfast. My tea is poured out by an Indian or a Chinese. My porridge is served by a Scottish farmer, or my corn flakes by Mr. Kellogg and his friends. My toast I accept at the hands of an English farmer who has joined hands with a baker. My marmalade is passed to me by a Spaniard, my banana by a West Indian. I am indebted to half the world before I have finished breakfast." The secret of half my happiness is that I belong to a world family.

To imagine life on the individual basis leads us to a situation which it is amusing to contemplate but would be no fun to realize. No clothes would be available save those we could make for ourselves, presumably from the skins of beasts, since, if we are not to have the fruits of other men's labors, nothing woven for us is available. We should sally out to try to procure breakfast with no weapon save that which we ourselves could fashion.

As I sit at my desk I realize that any good I can do through writing these words is a good only possible through the co-operation, literally, of hundreds of my brothers. I think of the pen with which I write, the electric light, the warmth of the fire, the friendly books on the shelves which line the room, the subsequent co-operation of publishers, printers, proofreaders, retailers, and travelers and a score of other helpers, without whom sending out this message would be impossible.

Shall we, then, receiving such untold benefit from our membership of the family, deem it unfair when we are asked to bear the consequences of the family ignorance, the family folly, the family sin? Shall I cry to God and say, "Why did you make a world like this?" when I have just decided that this is the best choice that lay before God himself, and that my best judgment confirms his choice?

These may seem hard words to some lonely sufferer, and in truth there is a greater word for him, as we shall see; but there is light for many in the thought that God was faced with a real alternative in making the basis of life that of the family or the unit, that the latter choice would have brought far more pain to the individual, and that selfishness would have been a greater evil than suffering. There would never be any happiness for a worthy individual in a private escape from suffering to which others were exposed. Solitary comforts are poor things. The very essence of our best self is love, and love wants to share not only pleasures but pain. Love would refuse an emancipation from pain which only included the self, just as love rejects the thought of salvation which is not available for every son of man. The thought which, for the noblest men and women on earth, would make life intolerable if carried into effect, is that they should be excluded totally from the pain of others.

Dr. Crichton-Miller, in his book *The New Psychology and the Preacher,*[3] gives an illustration which I have permission to reproduce here. An important express was about to leave a London terminus. An agitated lady assailed the stationmaster and begged him to postpone the departure of the train. He told her he had no power to do so, and that the only man who could was the general manager. She rushed to his office and repeated her request.

[3] (London: Jarrolds), p. 209.

"We have just heard," she said, "that our boy has met with a serious accident and is not expected to live. My husband is on his way, but he cannot possibly arrive until fifteen minutes after the hour of departure. If you keep the train waiting you will be giving him the only chance of seeing the boy alive. Surely if you have any spark of human sympathy you will not refuse!"

The general manager said, "Madam, I am very sorry for you and for your husband, but I cannot do it."

"You mean you won't do it," she said crossly. "You know very well that you could hold the train up if you wished to do so."

"Madam," he said, "the train makes more than one important connection which would be lost if I delayed it. There may be others in the train to whom the catching of one of these connections may mean just as much as to your husband. My business is to serve the community by maintaining the most trustworthy railway service that is possible."

There is a further word for the individual, a message which I think covers his individual problem; but our illustration does show us the only possible basis on which a train service can be run and—more importantly—the only possible basis on which a world can be run.

It is a commonplace to say that if two consequences both follow from a given proposition we cannot plaintively ask to have the one without the other, even though the one may strike us as pleasing and beneficial and the other seem evil and hurtful.[4]

This world is not a finished piece of work. God is still at work on it and in it. It is not yet "the best of all possible worlds" but it is the world of best possibilities. If we allow that the basis on which God has arranged human life is the best, we cannot com-

---

[4] I have taken some paragraphs here from an earlier book, *Why Do Men Suffer?* (Nashville: Abingdon Press, 1936, an Apex reprint).

plain at those inescapable, painful consequences which flow from that basis—even when they appear so distressing as to seem to deny the love and power of God—any more than we can applaud because God has provided man with that necessity of life which we call water, and then curse him because someone drowns; or praise him for the inestimable benefits of fire and curse him because someone is burnt by it.

One is left with the uncomfortable feeling that if all the resources of the human family were devoted to the cure and prevention of disease and mental suffering, the men who dream of landing on the moon could, within one generation, banish the amount of suffering which constitutes a problem.

Chapter 5

Is my suffering just a bit of bad luck?

IN ANSWERING THAT QUESTION EVERYTHING DEPENDS ON WHAT we mean by luck. We live in an ordered universe. Everything that happens has its cause—indeed, a whole string of causes. The universe is cosmos everywhere and chaos nowhere. Further, when we say that something is a chance happening or an accident or a piece of good or bad luck, we must not suppose that, however it may surprise *us,* God is also surprised. The Christian believes that God knows everything that happens and that he knew the future before it happened. Let it be quite clear, then, that God knew you were going to have this illness but, as we said in chapter 3, his knowing did not make it happen.

I am writing these words during a spell of bronchitis. God knew it would happen. But that knowing was not causative. The east wind and a cold church and a constitutional weakness going back to early childhood and bacilli in the respiratory passages were contributory causes, and God knew all about them and what they would bring upon me.

Now turn back to the matter of chance or luck. For myself I leave a place in my philosophy of life for chance happenings as long as I am allowed to define what I mean by chance or luck— and I mean by it an event which God did not intend and which man could not foresee. We have already seen that many things happen which God did not intend to happen. He allows many things which he did not intend. All sin is allowed, but not intended. Unless it were allowed man would have no free will. God allowed the sin a man did yesterday, but he knew it would happen before it did. But neither God's knowledge nor his allowing caused it to happen.

Every day thousands of things happen which could be called chance or accident or luck. I heard only recently of a golf ball badly driven by a beginner which struck a motorcyclist in the eye on an adjacent road. The cyclist swerved and a bus driver, in seeking to avoid the swerving cyclist, drove the bus off the road into a gully, where it turned over and injured half a dozen people. Unless we imagine that God ought to work a miracle to prevent all accidents—in which case man would never learn—then in a world made like this, accidents—defined as events which God did not intend and which man could not foresee—are inevitable. How foolish it would be for one of those bus passengers—even if stricken by blindness through splintered glass from the bus windows—to suppose that his disability was the will of God, or that God had ceased to be loving, or that man's folly was greater than God's power. How would man learn anything if his foolishness, carelessness, stupidity, ignorance, and sin were always overcome and safeguarded against evil consequences by some expression of interfering power on the part of omnipotence? To prevent, by a use of omnipotence, foolishness from producing its consequences, would fill the earth with unteachable fools. I do not deny that there are many things God *could* do by the use of his power. I suppose he could, in the illustration above, prevent the golf ball ever going off the fairway. (As a bad golfer I wish he would!) He could make the cyclist evade the ball, and so on. But more and more clearly I feel that while no one can answer the question as to what God can or cannot do, there are many things which God *must* not do, even though we wish he would, and we imagine that if only we had his power we would do them.

It is interesting to note that the more man learns about the laws by which God runs the universe the more he can exclude what we call luck. We toss up a coin and say that whether it falls heads or tails is purely a matter of luck. But if I knew all the factors involved in tossing up a coin—its weight, the number of revolutions it made, the air resistance, the force used, and so on—then presumably the way it fell could be calculated mathematically. The more man knows about the laws which govern the universe and the more wisely he acts as a result of his knowledge, the more will he be able to eliminate those "accidents" and "bad luck" which bring him disaster.

But I must guard against a faulty deduction some reader may make. He may feel, "Well, if one allows that an element of luck enters into life then anything may happen!" No! Anything cannot happen. I am quite sure of the most important fact that God has guarded this universe. Its laws are not infinite in number and therefore only a certain number of possible things can happen. Of course I don't know what this number is. Nobody does. The permutations and combinations of all the possibilities that could happen on a planet governed by laws which God ordained are beyond the scope of man's mind. Perhaps if some brilliant supermathematician knew all the laws and all the possibilities, he could work out the sum, but by faith in the wisdom and love of God—not by any scientific guess—I am quite sure that there are only a certain number of things that can happen.

To see this, let us go back to the parable of the nursery. The parents who allow their child to stumble and fall in it as he learns to walk do not, we said, put eiderdowns on the floor and have the walls padded. Even then the child can get a nasty tumble. He

41

can hurt himself fairly badly. *But the parents have excluded razor blades and bottles of sulphuric acid and arsenic.* In other words, they have guarded the nursery. It is not true to say that *anything* might happen. *Nothing can possibly happen with which the child, in co-operation with loving parents, cannot cope as he learns to walk.* Nothing can happen from which he cannot win a definite gain. I believe that the whole environment of man is guarded by our loving Father in the same way. Some terrible things can happen, but it is not true to say that *anything* can happen. Nothing can possibly happen from which gain cannot be won. Nothing can possibly happen with which it is utterly beyond our powers to cope.

If a thing happens to you, therefore, God knows all about it. He knows it can happen, that it is going to happen, that it has happened. But he knows also that nothing can possibly happen in this nursery of a universe that of itself has power to defeat his own purposes, and that if man grasps his opportunities and uses his resources and seeks also his Father's aid—just as a child might stretch up a hand when he stumbles—real good can be won from everything that seems like unfortunate accident. From that fact a profound truth emerges to me: the apparent evil in any happening that can occur to man is the measure of God's challenge to man to transform it into advantage. If the measure of the supposed evil becomes the measure of our right reaction, it will be the measure of our gain from anything which God allows. No happening would be allowed if it could defeat God, just as razor blades and acid would not be allowed in a nursery by the most Spartan parent.

Look at it like this. Man is very proud of what he calls his scientific discoveries—and indeed they are tremendous. But from a religious point of view it is true to say that he can discover nothing unless God reveals it. What the scientist discovers, God allows him to discover. The progress of the scientist's mind which allows him, benefiting from the discoveries of his predecessors, to startle the world with some new discovery is only an unveiling of one of the secrets of God by God himself, and *man never made a discovery until he was in sight of power to cope with that discovery.* If we could bring back our great-great-great-grandfathers and put them in the modern world, their sanity would be overturned. They would find that coping with the modern world was more than they could manage, for their minds would be utterly unattuned to its demands. Man has slowly climbed to his discoveries, and they have become discoveries only when he could use them for the happiness of his fellows and the glory of God. Yes, I know you are thinking of atomic energy. So am I. But don't let the horror of it disguise the fact that it *can* be used in man's service, even in his highest service. And here again the measure of the wonder of the discovery is God's challenge that it be used in his service. God is trusting us to use all new discoveries to further his plans.

So there are no accidents or chance happenings or bits of luck that are outside the scope of God's knowledge and man's power to deal with them adequately. Nothing can ever happen to us but that in co-operation with God we can turn it into a spiritual gain. I mean that literally. Do not just meet the liability with an asset that is its equivalent, but turn the liability itself into an asset. So don't say, "Well, it's just a matter of luck, and all life is chance, and instead of purpose there are accidents." Remember the parable of the nursery. Nothing is allowed to happen that could ultimately defeat the purposes of God.

As I have thought about the problem of the place of chance in the Christian life, I have found a kind of daydream taking shape in my mind. It has seemed to me as though a number of people were scattered through the length of a muddy lane, along which a laborer with a cart full of broken pieces of tile slowly passed, and to each person he gave a spadeful of fragments, which somehow the recipient knew he had to fit together into a pattern and the pattern into a pavement. In my dream many cried out to the laborer and said that of all those broken pieces of ill-assorted shapes and sizes they could make hardly any use at all, let alone make something beautiful. Then I saw in my dream that the more thoughtful people turned the fragments over, or exchanged some of theirs for others doled out to the people near them, and getting together made not only a beautiful pattern, but a firm pavement where there had been mud. It was a strange dream. The people who moved in its shadows complained loudly of injustice, for some got beautiful, colored stones, and these lucky people were able at once to make them into a pattern and set the pattern into the pavement. But others got rough-edged stones, dull of color, and they complained bitterly of their bad luck. But in my dream joy came to my heart when some of the most humble people who said nothing, heard, as from an angel voice, the advice, "Turn them over!" and on doing so found they were holding precious stones.

I could not help feeling that somehow life is like that. This man has good luck, and that man has bad luck, but I wonder whether, in the sight of God, there is any real difference between good luck and bad luck. So often the latter is a frozen asset which ultimately brings immense spiritual wealth. Dives thought he had good luck and Lazarus bad, but in the next world things looked very different (Luke 16:19-31), and—if we *must* use time words—we shall be longer there than here. I would like you to think about that. Life cannot ultimately be unjust. I have seen the lucky ones finish their lives having made a very poor thing of their luck, and I have seen the unlucky ones turn the rough stones of ill luck over and find they were jewels, and turn the things we call calamities into a pattern of loveliness and a pathway for other feet. I think it is God's purpose that the lucky ones and the unlucky ones should make a pattern and a pavement, and cry out at last with Jeremy Taylor:

> Lord, come away;
> Why dost Thou stay?
> Thy road is ready and Thy paths made straight
> With longing expectation wait
> The consecration of Thy beauteous feet.

For "All things work together for good to them that love God" (Rom. 8:28 K.J.V.) or, as C. H. Dodd translates the famous text, "In everything . . . he [God] co-operates for good with those who love God" (N.E.B.).

Your illness may be bad luck, in the sense defined. It is something God did not intend and you could not foresee. But it cannot of itself defeat God's final purposes, nor has it in itself any power to defeat you. It contains a challenge which, rightly responded to, can bring treasure.

Chapter 6

Where do God's goodness and omnipotence come in?

IT IS VERY NATURAL THAT A SUFFERER SHOULD WONDER WHY, if God has immeasurable power and infinite goodness, he does not either prevent disease and calamity or else do something quickly remedial when they overtake us. Many men and women in their hearts have felt as the philosopher John Stuart Mill felt. If God is good, the suffering in the world must mean that it happens because he cannot help it. In that case he is not all-powerful. If he is all-powerful and does not prevent or speedily end it, it must be because he is not good. So, runs the argument, either he is all-powerful and not good, or good but not all-powerful. He cannot be both.

Let us look at this problem.

First of all I am myself driven to the belief that God is good. The reason which most convinces me is that man at his best is good. The reader of this book is good. He or she would not smite a child with cancer or wreck his life with polio or insanity. Indeed, I can say with safety that the reader of this book is unlikely to do anything deliberately cruel or unkind. If we do fall into unkindness, cruelty, or what we call "sin," we reproach ourselves. We know, if we know anything at all, that goodness is better than badness; kindness is better than cruelty; love is better than lust; self-denial and sacrifice are better than self-aggression and selfishness. If there is a God at all, his nature must contain and express all those good things. If his nature does not contain them, then we, his creatures, are better than he is, for we despise the opposites to, or absence of, the good. We may not as yet be able to *see,* as the work of a good God, many things he does and allows any more than a tiny boy whose father is a surgeon can see it to be a good thing to make a patient unconscious and then stretch him out on a table and cut him open with a knife. But the child who knows his father's nature from other evidence has to leave that problem in abeyance, awaiting further light, and he has to hold on to the fact that his father is good and is doing good. So, when Christ tells us that God is good, when Christ lives a good life himself and tells us that God is like that, we have to hold many things like disease in abeyance, awaiting further light, and we have to hold on to the fact that it is impossible to believe that God is evil. If he is, where does goodness come from? We have replaced the mystery of evil by a greater mystery of good.

There is, of course, another alternative, and that is that God is well-meaning and also very powerful, but stupid. I do not think we need stay on that point. All man's discoveries are divine revelations and no one is going to believe that this amazing universe, the discoveries about which nearly take our breath away, if it came from a divine hand at all, was made by an intensely powerful imbecile!

Is it then that God is not as powerful as we thought; that he cannot help the suffering that overtakes us? Yet surely one fleeting thought of the power of wind and wave, of flashing lightning and tearing hurricane, of volcano and earthquake,[1] apart altogether from the terrifying energy locked up in the atom, con-

---

[1] I have discussed the suffering that follows natural disasters in *Why Do Men Suffer?* *op. cit.,* pp. 89-105.

47

vince us that the creator of this universe could fitly be called the Lord of power.

But here we must consider the whole question of the nature of power. I think the concept of power is misunderstood because we imagine it to mean ability to do anything. Let us make up another illustration from the hockey field. Let us suppose that you and I are on the sidelines watching a game—which I must confess I love to do—and a huge giant of a man who is completely ignorant of the game comes along and asks what all the struggle is about. Supposing someone tells him that it is an effort to get the ball into the net, either at one end or the other. Supposing that, thinking to please, the giant stalks onto the field, knocks men right and left, picks up the ball, brushes off the goalkeeper, and puts it into the net. What a riot there would be! And what an interfering so-and-so the giant would be called! And what would happen to the game of hockey if that sort of behavior occurred?

You may think it a foolish illustration, but think back in imagination to 1665 when the great plague was raging. How many prayed that it should end! How many people must have prayed God to walk off the sidelines, as it were, and end men's struggle! Many prayers must have ascended that this or that individual might be healed. But if those prayers had been answered *plague would have been with us still*. Men would never have bothered to find out the causes and thus *prevent* plague. They would have put a prayer in the slot, so to speak, and drawn out a cure. We shall ask in a subsequent chapter why the germs of diseases were ever created at all; but part of the game of life is man's struggle for mastery, and to end the struggle by a show of what is popularly thought of as "omnipotence" makes the game —and all man learns from it—meaningless.

48

Of course, this solves nothing in regard to the *origin* of disease. It only pushes the problem far enough back to absolve man from responsibility *for* its origin.[4] Some have speculated that there may have been a species of "fall" amongst men who are now extinct but who were once higher in attainment, both spiritually and physically, than anything to which man as we know him has ever attained since, and that the wickedness of these supermen originally brought chaos and disease into the world. For myself, I know of no real support for this theory, which seems determined to saddle man with a responsibility for disease which the facts do not warrant. Others believe that the world was full of spiritual intelligences even more closely in the image of God than man is and that they morally "fell" and became evil intelligences— hence the devil and his angels—which brought havoc into God's world and upset his plans; evil intelligences who had earlier derived from God enough power to create those forms of life like—say—the hooded cobra, the giant squid, and the polio virus, which now pester man. But for this speculation I find little support and no attractiveness.

2. A view to which I think we are driven is that the world was not created with only man's freedom from danger and suffering in view. One dreams of a Utopia in which "the wolf shall dwell with the lamb, and the leopard shall lie down with the kid" and the child can touch a deadly snake without fear (Isa. 11:6-9). And it may be that we shall reach that state one day. In the meantime, the world of created animals, including man, looks like a vast arena where each organism must fight for its existence,

[4] I am afraid John Wesley was wrong when in his preface to *Primitive Physic* he argues, "Why is there pain in the world?" and answers, "Because there is sin. Had there been no sin, there would have been no pain. Pain is the necessary effect of sin." (London: Epworth Press, 1960.)

and Jesus seems to have recognized that no divine protection stopped the wolf from snatching the lamb if it could do so (John 10:12). When a lion carries off a missionary, Christian people find it at once a problem that God should let it happen, but the psalmist sings:

> The high mountains are for the wild goats;
>   the rocks are a refuge for the badgers.
>
> . . . .
>
> Thou makest darkness, and it is night,
>   when all the beasts of the forest creep forth.
> The young lions roar for their prey,
>   seeking their food from God.
>
> —Ps. 104:18, 20-21

The Christian prays that the lions, young or old, will keep away from missionaries, but there is more than humor in this limerick:

> There was a young lady of Ryde
> Who was carried away by the tide,
>   But a man-eating shark
>   Was heard to remark,
> "I knew that the Lord would provide."

And seriously, man must realize that every organism in the world including himself is fighting for its life, seeking its food that it may continue to live.

Not many centuries ago, in this my "island home," wolves came down in winter from the forests on the hilltops, and, unable to find their normal food, attacked villagers who had to fight them and destroy them or they would themselves have been destroyed, together with their sheep, cattle, and poultry. Even as I was writing these words, *The Times* reported as follows from Spain:

Nearly all the dogs of the village of Lubian, in Zamora province, have been killed by a pack of wolves.

Apparently reduced to extreme hunger, the wolves without fear of anything or anybody, according to a report from Zamora, came down from their lairs in the snow-covered mountains during the night and roamed around the streets of Lubian. They broke into corrals and killed virtually all the watchdogs in the village.

The mountains to the north of Zamora, which form a labyrinth of peaks and ridges, valleys and ravines, are known for their many wolves. Every winter hunting parties are organized by the authorities to protect the sheep, cattle, and poultry from their raids, prizes being awarded to the hunters who bag the highest number.[5]

Still the fight goes on. Many diseases are caused by germs or more minute organisms. We have all heard of a virus infection. Our commonest enemies now are smaller than wolves. We may not shoot them as our forefathers shot the wolves, but the battle is the same and the problem is the same. It is the battle man fights for survival.

Man has been told that he is to rule supreme in the creation. "Let them have dominion over the fish of the sea, and over the birds of the air, and over the cattle, and over all the earth, and over every creeping thing that creeps upon the earth" (Gen. 1:26); but he has had to fight for that dominion and the battle still goes on. The psalmist cries that man is to have authority over all sheep and oxen, the beasts of the field, the fowl of the air, the fish of the sea, and all the works of God's hands (Ps. 8:6-8),

---

[5] *The Times* (London), December 23, 1961. Reprinted by permission of *The Times.*

and those who are vegetarians on principle have to remember that Jesus went fishing with his men and is reported more than once to have prepared a meal of fish for his disciples.[6] But to have *authority* over an enemy does not mean that the desired *power* over him has been reached, as any policeman thinking of the criminals who elude him would be quick to acknowledge. He has authority but not power. (One wishes that one's conscience had as much power as it has authority!) How true and salutary is that wise word in the Epistle to the Hebrews, "We do not yet see everything in subjection to him" (Heb. 2:8). That word "yet" hints at a glorious possibility, but in the meantime man's battle for supremacy must go forward and he will learn more in the battle than if all were done for him, just as the hockey player in our illustration learns by playing the game, not by having someone put the ball in the net by irresistible power.

3. There is, however, a view about germs which I think may be part of the answer to the question, "Why were the germs of disease ever created?"

Most people know that the human body contains bacteria—which are healthy and friendly to man. They are called saprophytes. Some of them live in, and feed on, the various secretions of the body. Most people also know that the very chemical constitution of the secretions of the body can be altered by the emotions of the deep mind. It was found, for example, that when a nursing mother who was breast-feeding her baby was forced to watch a fight between her husband whom she loved and a man who had attempted to seduce her and whom she hated, the hate in the mother's mind was of such intensity that

[6] Matt. 14:17; 15:34; Mark 6:38; 8:7; Luke 5:6; 9:13; John 6:9; 21:6; and especially 21:9-13.

her breast milk was turned to poison and the baby fell dead from her breast.[7]

Dr. H. P. Newsholme, formerly Medical Officer of Health for Birmingham, with whom I talked and corresponded on this point, agrees in his famous book, *Health, Disease and Integration,* that "there is no essential difference in mechanism between the secretion of milk by the breast glands and the secretion of saliva by the salivary glands and *of mucus by the mucous glands.*" (Italics mine.)

During a lecture at Cambridge I heard a most interesting story of which I made notes:

Dr. Harold Wolff and Dr. Stewart Wolf of Cornell University in America experimented on a willing patient called Tom who was employed in their hospital. As a result of an accident years earlier, Tom had to feed himself through a specially constructed opening directly into his stomach *which could be observed.*

Tom was told he was being dismissed for inefficiency. Not only did his face grow red and angry but the lining of his stomach became congested and engorged with blood even to the point of bleeding at the merest touch. When he was told that the alleged dismissal had been concocted, his stomach returned to normal. Further experiments showed that if Tom was depressed and dejected his stomach became gray and covered with mucus.

Dr. Stafford-Clark tells of a cat who was induced to eat a meal containing barium so that in X rays the outline of stomach and digestive organs could plainly be seen on a screen. When a dog was brought into the room and the cat securely held "the whole contour and behaviour of its stomach altered completely, the

---

[7] See Eric Pritchard in *Infant Education,* quoted by Dr. H. P. Newsholme in *Health, Disease and Integration* (London: Allen and Unwin), p. 55.

valves at each end closed tight while the rest of the stomach sagged and digestive movements ceased." [8]

Emotion, therefore, especially if intense, and/or long sustained, can produce chemical and other changes in the saliva or *the mucus* which covers certain tissues. With this in mind I want to quote from the researches of Dr. J. G. Adami. He writes:

> Every pathogenic microbe has closely related forms or species differing from it in little beyond the fact that the one is virulent, the other non-virulent. Next, it is to be noted that these allied species are found suggestively growing in the cavities or on the mucous surfaces of the body, in the same habitat as the virulent forms, or again in water and foodstuffs. . . . This state of affairs in itself leads to the conclusion that pathogenic microbes at some period, or periods, have originated from the microbes saprophytic upon [=friendly to] the body surfaces, or existing commonly in the water and foodstuffs; that they have originated by adaptation of these forms to growth, not merely on, but within the tissues.

He writes again, "According to the environment so do bacteria assume special qualities." [9]

What does all this amount to in simple English? To this, I think: that germs, friendly to human health and feeding happily on mucus and other secretions within us, find that, through our emotional reactions, the nature and composition of these secretions alters and becomes unsuitable to them. They therefore naturally move to some other feeding ground where they find food but where their activities interfere with our health and well-being. From being benign baccilli, therefore, they become malign. But

[8] David Stafford-Clark, *Psychiatry Today* (Baltimore: Penguin Books, 1959, a Pelican Book), p. 238. Dr. Clark also verifies the story of Tom.

[9] *Medical Contributions to the Study of Evolution* (London: Duckworth, 1918), pp. 23, 42.

if man has himself changed the composition of his own secretions by harboring emotions like excessive worry or guilt or resentment or hate, and has thus driven friendly germs to become hostile germs, he can hardly cry out petulantly to God, "I don't know why you ever created these enemies of my peace." I find it very, very hard to believe that the germ or baccillus of smallpox was once a friendly little fellow ministering to my total health, and the idea that *all* the germs of disease were once friendly and benign has not been put forward by anyone; but, before we pass on, listen to Dr. Adami on the germ of diphtheria.

Diptheria gains its simplest explanation as being due to the acquirement within recent times of virulent properties by some *previously harmless* diphtheroid bacillus growing in the throat and upper respiratory passages. And so it has been with . . . infections in general. . . . I admit that there may be contradictory causes, that particular environments may favour the origin or reappearance of particular diseases, as again that local tissue environment may determine particular selective development of virulence.[10]

Dr. Newsholme himself went so far as to say that

nervous activity arising from *primary acute emotion* or from cerebral irritation, may conceivably produce living particulate enzymes or "viruses" capable of causing catabolism[11] and capable of conveying "disease" to the individual and to others. In other words, the "filtrable virus" need not necessarily be derived from a source, always the same, external to the body, but may be the product of the unhealthy body itself.[12]

It will be interesting if, after death, we are allowed to ask

[10] J. G. Adami, *op cit.*, p. 42.
[11] Catabolism means the breaking down and destruction of the cells of the body.
[12] Dr. H. P. Newsholme, *Health, Disease and Integration, op. cit.*, p. 68.

questions and challenge God with making disease germs, to learn
that man is himself responsible for the virulence and hostility
of some of them. One begins to wonder and speculate whether
many forms of life, which in the evolutionary scale are below man
and which develop hostility to him, may be prisons in which
spirit-entities express some primitive striving or some anger
against conditions for which man is responsible! The saints sometimes seem able to make friends even with leopards.[18]

Alas, in every field of human inquiry there is so little that we
know. When, during the First World War, I served in Mesopo-
tamia as an officer in the Indian army and later as a chaplain,
disease was a greater enemy than the Turks and cost us more
men's lives. We used to curse the sandflies which brought us down
in hundreds with a particular brand of fever. I remember how
lustily the men going on leave would sing a chorus which went:

> I wouldn't choose
> To live with the Jews
>   Or the Arab tribes we see.
> Farewell, little hell,
>   Sandfly, goodbye.
> There's a Blighty girl waiting for me.

But the "Arab tribes" (who, be it noted, seemed not to suffer
from the bites of these tiny demons) said, "Sandflies are our
friends. They fertilize our date palms. No sandflies, no dates."

I would willingly, at one time, have consigned all wasps to
perdition. But a well-qualified writer in *The Times* wrote,

[18] See my *His Life and Ours* (Nashville: Abingdon Press, 1933, 1961), pp. 98-
100.

Nine tenths of the activities of wasps are beneficent to man. From late spring to early autumn they seek out and destroy vast multitudes of caterpillars and grubs, which, if left unchecked, would destroy our crops, our vegetables, our orchards, and our trees.[14]

Do we know enough about germs and viruses to say that all their activities are, from our point of view, evil? Would human life be more difficult without them?

This does not stop me from "swatting" a wasp in my study or from trying to murder disease germs in my body, but it lights up a point of view which should be included as we try to work out a Christian philosophy of suffering.

It is incredible that God is responsible for the creation of anything essentially evil. That God, as it were, sat down one afternoon and thought out, planned, and created a virus which later, multiplied by thousands, would torment, wreck the happiness of, and perhaps painfully kill an innocent and lovely baby is impossible of belief by anyone of undistorted mind.

That God is still at work in his world, that he is hindered, possibly by nonhuman, nonincarnate evil intelligences, and certainly by human ignorance, folly, and sin, that much which he planned as good has been turned into temporary evil in the terrific struggle going on in every part of his creation, and that man has not yet found his proper place in the universe, all this does seem a possible clue where so much is dark.

One thing is clear. We must ally ourselves with God in every way open to us, knowing that our complete health is his ideal will and that even if for a dozen reasons we do not win back physical wholeness he will let nothing be lost; and that we *can* turn what

---

[14] August 22, 1934.

is not his will into his ultimate glory and our ultimate gain. "The team" will win the game. The victory is promised on what Livingstone called "the word of a Gentleman," and our private sorrows and suffering, however sore now, desolating to our present faith, and puzzling to the intellect, will finally form such a glowing part of God's victory, that joy will fill our hearts. So far from everlastingly complaining, we shall be saying, "Fancy God being able to make *that* out of my pain! Blessed be his glorious name forever."

Chapter 9

How can I fight this illness?

My old friend and teacher, from whom I learned so much, the late Rev. Dr. W. R. Maltby, used to say: "It is not wicked to be ill, but it is wicked to be more ill than you need be." What a true word that is! Illness means that we can serve the community with less efficiency and possibly hinder those who look after us from fullness of life and service. I hope that does not sound unkind. I know that the invalid who prays and loves and offers his suffering to God does far more good in the world than thousands of fit and healthy people do, but he doesn't *have* to be ill before he can pray and love and offer himself to God. Jesus said, "I have come that men may have life, and may have it in all its fullness." (John 10:10 N.E.B.) Would John Wesley, who prayed and loved and endlessly toiled for the greater part of a century, have done more if, physically handicapped, he had prayed in his bedroom? It is hard to answer perhaps, but I adhere to my first principle that God's ideal will is complete fitness of body, mind, and spirit. Let me offer God as fit an instrument as I can for his service! Paul says, "I beseech you therefore, brethren, by the mercies of God, to present your bodies a living sacrifice, holy [healthy], well-pleasing to God which is your spiritual worship." (Rom. 12:1, English Revised Version margin.) In other words, maximum spiritual service can ideally be rendered if one has a healthy body and a sound mind dedicated to God.

I can safely suppose that any reader of this chapter who is ill has called in his doctor. The doctor's training includes all that has been usefully learned about healing the body and mind since Hippocrates, who lived about 450 B.C. At the same time no good doctor pretends that he has thought of everything. Nor will he object to "another's opinion" being sought. Consultants have been derided for "knowing more and more about less and less," but I can speak from experience of inestimable help being usually given by them.

Osteopaths are derided too, but again I can speak from experience of weeks of pain, including the pain, discomfort, and time-consuming nuisance of hot poultices applied every few hours—ended in half an hour by adequate osteopathy, and just recently, when a young woman was referred to me because her pain was supposed to be "psychological," a medically qualified osteopath found a partially dislocated hip, and in my presence relieved her of pain in a few minutes though she had had months of fussing with steel belts, plaster jackets, and rest, including weeks of lying on her back.

If I were ill I would turn to anyone who could put me right if I trusted him enough to feel that he would not make matters worse; and in my opinion there is a place for the psychiatrist, the dietitian, the nature-cure therapist, the manipulator, and for treament by radiesthesia or, as I prefer to call it, odic force.[1] As for the physiotherapist, the masseuse, and the efficient and conscientious nurse, I can think of no more worthwhile job for a young woman to take up. Such a person, properly trained and qualified, renders a tremendous service to the community.

But when all such help has been considered is there nothing

[1] I have described odic force and given instances of its successful use in my book, *Wounded Spirits* to be published by Abingdon Press in 1963.

else to be done? What about religion, with its emphasis on faith and prayer? Do we not read of "faith healing" and of healing through prayer?

I must not repeat here what I have written in other books on this subject,[2] but some simple things may be said.

In my opinion, by far the best way for the sufferer to think out the relationship of religion to his suffering would be for him to ask an instructed minister or clergyman whom he trusted to visit him. This would give him an opportunity for confession—if this were felt necessary—and for discussion.

It could not be anything but a contribution to the regaining of health for a sufferer to make sure that his religious life was in good order. We all know in these days to what an extent the bottling up of hate or fear or resentment or worry or malice or guilt can set off illness and delay recovery from illnesses that have a physical origin. Doctors too are increasingly aware of this. They now do not only ask the patient with a gastric ulcer what he has been eating; they ask him what he is worrying about. Ministers could do a great service to patients—since we have all sinned—in declaring the loving forgiveness of God and making sure that the patient not only assents but *receives* into the depths of his mind that healing truth.

Prayer for healing is to be encouraged as long as the patient understands clearly what he is doing, or, if prayer is made for him in church, what intercession aims at doing for him. It aims to bring the patient into as complete a unity with God as is

[2] *Why Do Men Suffer?*; *Prescription for Anxiety*; *Psychology, Religion, and Healing*; *Psychology and Life* (Abingdon Press). *Psychology in Service of the Soul* (Epworth Press). *Wounded Spirits* (to be published by Abingdon Press in 1963).

possible. Clearly it follows the reception of forgiveness. Equally clearly prayer is not a cure-all. It frequently fails to cure because it is not the relevant way of healing that particular illness. It will not be wasted, but frankly it does not usually bring physical cure. You would not say, "O God make me better," if you had a toothache. You would go to the dentist. Do we really expect God to deliver us from an illness which may have a similarly physical origin just because we do not know the relevant person to whom to go? But health is harmonious correspondence with environment; the body with the physical world, the mind with the world of true ideas, and the soul with God. Prayer at any rate can bring health to the soul, and the interrelation of body, mind, and spirit is so close that health in one relationship indubitably increases total health, and if the dis-ease, even though physically suffered, is an expression of a spiritual or emotional malaise, prayer, with the reconciliation with God which it brings, could well be the main therapeutic factor.

In regard to faith a lot of misunderstanding is current. We are told by some to "have faith," as if one could do so like turning on a tap. We fit and healthy people only make others feel guilty and miserable by telling them to "have faith." *Christ knew how to call out faith.* We so rarely do that for people. I dislike the term "faith healing," for some "healers" make us feel that if only we had faith we could be cured of anything. This, I think, is nonsense. It must be most comforting to some "faith healers" to move about the country holding missions. If people are healed or their symptoms removed (often only temporarily, though this is not publicized), then the healer adds them to his list of successes. If the patients are unhealed (and thus driven into a deeper depression than ever), then it is because they had insufficient "faith." Heads the healer wins, tails the patient loses! In such missions the determining factor, if the patient appears healed, is often not true faith at all but a species of accidental suggestibility which is part of the patient's temperamental makeup and no more a credit or discredit to him than the fact that he has a long nose or ginger hair.

True faith in this connection is a different thing altogether and has nothing whatever to do with believing theological propositions. What did the people whom Jesus healed know of theology? Professor Macmurray says that "Christ's use of the term 'faith' does not allow us to take it as the equivalent of 'belief' in the ordinary sense of holding certain views." Believing *in* a person is quite a different thing from believing the truth of propositions about him, and it is the former that is so essential. Christ's words, his very voice, his eyes, his quiet authority, and the lovely life he lived would make men know intuitively that they could trust him, that they were accepted just as they were. The word "faith" should always be reserved for *a person*. To talk of having "faith" in castor oil or some other material thing is, in my view, a misuse of language.

Faith, then, is quietly trusting the God who is like Jesus *whether one is healed or not,* knowing that we are safe, that God loves us, is at work in us and through us, and will use the suffering, if, for various reasons, it cannot yet be ended. We *can* have that kind of faith by constantly looking at him as the Gospels teach us to regard him, and by talking with him, listening, looking, and loving. In that utterly reliable and loving presence the querulous, rebellious complaint dies. We still want to be well but we can bear the delay even if complete healing only comes after death, when we throw off, like a tattered old overcoat, the physical covering of a spirit that without hindrance enters joyously into the heritage of that health which has always been God's will.[3]

---

[3] Those who want an excellent essay on true faith and its relevance to our subject would find it in a shilling pamphlet by Dr. Denis V. Martin, called, *The Meaning of Faith in Faith-Healing* (London: Epworth Press, 1954). There is also a chapter on "The Nature and Place of Faith in Faith Healing" in my *Psychology, Religion, and Healing, op. cit.*, p. 423, and a chapter entitled "The Weapon of Faith" in *Why Do Men Suffer? op cit.*, pp. 164 ff.

Appendix to Chapter 9

Healing Missions

I feel that I must warn the sufferer against missions and meetings and services held by various kinds of "healers" because they have done so much harm to people I know that I feel very strongly about them, though I will summarize here views which I have expressed more fully elsewhere.[4]

There can be no objection to a quiet service, with or without the laying on of hands, in the presence of the patient's relatives or a few carefully selected friends. But the patient should be instructed beforehand by the ministrant so that if disappointed by the continuance of his illness, he does not lose faith or make mistaken deductions about faith and about God.

Healing services open to the general public are not allowed in Methodist churches by a resolution of the Methodist Conference of 1952. The reasons I gave when proposing this resolution may be summarized as follows:

A. *Emotional Perils*

1. It is impossible for a large number of sick people to be gathered in a congregation and invited to come forward for healing without intense emotion being aroused in both the patients and the onlookers. This has frequently resulted in outbreaks of hysteria, with terrifying results for all.

2. A few people may claim to be healed there and then, though in two much-advertised and crowded "healing missions" in Liver-

[4] *Psychology, Religion, and Healing, op. cit.,* and *Wounded Spirits, op. cit.*

pool and Birkenhead some years ago no one even claimed healing.[5] Those who claim healing thrust the unhealed into a grim disappointment and share it themselves when, as so often happens, the apparently healed relapse into illness again, a fact not advertised by anyone and as far as possible concealed from everyone.

3. There is fostered a confusion between faith and suggestibility. The unhealed feel that they had insufficient faith and the healed congratulate themselves on having it, when the differentiating factor is often suggestibility, which is a temperamental quality we either have or have not; whereas true faith is a splendid quality which has to be worked for and *which does not necessarily insure healing*. We can have true faith without healing and we can have healing without faith.

4. Other faulty conclusions are secretly accepted by the unhealed, such as that religion is "no good," or that God has favorites, or that they themselves are unworthy. None of these conclusions is sound.

B. *Physical Perils*

1. The postponement of surgical help while waiting for the "healer" to visit the patient's area can render the surgeon's task harder or even impossible.

2. The transitory nature of the relief and the return of the symptoms increases the depression of the patient and lowers his morale in his fight for health.

3. The lack of discrimination on the part of the healer, such as in a case known to me of a little fellow with a club foot being promised football boots after his visit to a "healer," so that he

[5] *Birkenhead News*, June 10, 1939.

could play like other boys. His mental state on returning unhealed makes one angry about the whole farce. It should be remembered that Christ has more in common with the modern surgeon than with some faith healers, for he knew what was the matter and altered his treatment accordingly, whereas some healers lay hands on everyone without knowledge or insight and sometimes, by implication, blame the unhealed for not "having faith."

4. Most importantly, in certain cases of psychosomatic illness, the *symptom* of disease is banished and seen no more after the healing service. Thereupon a cure is announced and everybody is deeply impressed. But, *if the psychological condition which set up the symptom in the first place is not dealt with and healed, the unconscious mind will produce another symptom far more difficult to cure, or else set up mental or emotional symptoms which had been finding a certain expression in the physical ones.*

This truth lies behind Christ's words, which sound so stern, spoken to the man whom he cured by the pool of Bethesda, "Now that you are well again, leave your sinful ways, or you may suffer something worse" (John 5:14 N.E.B.). If the man's illness had been psychosomatic, a translation of inner guilt into bodily illness, then the unconscious mind would not repeat the same symptoms; it would find another so that its bluff could not easily be called and its activities be obvious. Jesus is not *threatening* the man, "Sin no more, that nothing worse befall you." He is stating a truth which anyone who has followed up the activities of "healing missions" could illustrate. For instance: "a duodenal ulcer is in many cases a substitute for conscious anxiety." [6] If the ulcer alone is "cured," the deep mind will either produce a more serious symptom, or else the anxiety will be expressed as conscious terror

[6] Arthur Guirdham, *A Theory of Disease* (London: Allen and Unwin, 1957), p. 88.

which is much harder to bear. It is easier to bear our sufferings in the body than in the mind. Many patients whose physical symptoms expressed mental dis-ease, have, after having merely the symptom cured, fallen into mental illness or "nervous breakdown."

Canon Grensted in his Bampton Lectures wrote:

The great danger of missions of healing is that by their very prestige and by their impressive setting they act with immense power along these (hysteria-producing) lines. They attract and profoundly affect hysterics of all kinds. But they give little guarantee that the cures achieved are radical. Even if the patients develop a new and edifying piety, this may easily be nothing more than a new phase of their hysteria, as far removed from true religion as fantasy is from fact.[7]

5. A fifth and very serious objection to the healing mission is that it encourages the patient to use God as a means of getting well, with the only too well-evidenced likelihood that if he recovers he will forget God. This puts God in the same category as a treatment. "Deep X ray failed, penicillin was ineffective, let's try religion." A man actually said to me, "I tried everything else so I thought I'd try a spot of prayer!" But it seems to me a serious heresy to regard God as a means to our end. We are means to his. The aim of prayer is hardly the same as the aim of a pill.

[7] I cannot refrain here from quoting further from Canon Grensted's Bampton Lectures: "To cure the symptom only invites the appearance of other symptoms which may be at least as serious. The story is told of a doctor who by repeated suggestion cured a patient of the conviction that he was a dog. The cure was reported triumphantly with the appended note, 'Unfortunately he now believes that he is a water-rat.' Of an enormous number of religious healings the same criticism must be made." L. W. Grensted, Oriel Professor of the Philosophy of the Christian Religion in the University of Oxford, *Psychology and God* (London: Longmans, Green & Co. Ltd., 1930), p. 117.

Those who desire healing through religion should sincerely seek to be forgiven and to get a new realization of the love and power of God. If healing comes, it will be a by-product and of course is to be welcomed. But we must face the fact that if we are honest we are far more interested in the health of our bodies than in that of our souls. We would far rather be cured of our cancer than of our meannesses, lusts, and hypocrisy. But we must not suppose that God's order of importance is the same as ours.

Some will feel that I am hard on "healing missions" and will quote the New Testament in support of them, pointing out that Christ healed people in the street. I would reply that repeatedly Christ sought privacy for his healings and after a healing told the patient, "Tell no man!" Consider Matt. 8:4 K.J.V., "See thou tell no man"; Matt. 9:30 K.J.V., "See that no man know it"; Mark 5:43 K.J.V., "He charged them . . . that no man should know it"; Mark 7:24 K.J.V., "[He] would have no man know it"; Mark 7:36 K.J.V., "He charged them that they should tell no man"; and Mark 8:30; 9:9; and so on. Jesus sent a leper to the priest so that he could get his "discharge certificate" but added, "Tell no man" (Luke 5:14 K.J.V.).

As for Christ healing in the street, I feel that this is no precedent for the modern church. Christ was Christ. He had insight and *knew* what was wrong with a patient without being told. He changed his technique accordingly. He knew whom he could heal and whom he couldn't. No one surely believes that Christ could have given sight to a man whose eyes had been gouged out, or healed the lameness of a man with a missing leg, and so on. Many illnesses with which ignorant healers try to deal are in the same category.

How different from Christ's methods is the setup of the healing mission of today. At its worst there is much advertisement beforehand. Patients, *whatever their disease,* are encouraged to come many miles. Soft music or the repetition of sentimental hymn tunes intentionally works up the emotion. The healer enters dramatically (with appropriate comments in the press later about his or her dress and "wonderful hands," etc.) and the performance begins. The "healer" does not understand one thing about anatomy, psychology, disease, or medicine; and without any sifting of cases, or variations in technique, or previous consultation with the doctor, or talk with the patient, he lays hands on the *head* of every kneeling suppliant. If the healer possesses "odic force" or if the patient is highly suggestible and has hysterical symptoms, there may be the appearance of a cure. This is blazoned next day in the press, which I have never known to report the frequent relapses in which mental depression is added to the return of the symptoms.

For myself I am glad that the Methodist Church, to which I belong, has banned from its premises such travesties, such exhibitions of primitive mumbo-jumbo. I believe in faith, but we do not live in the first century when faith was a projection from credulity. We live in a scientific age when faith is a projection from science; a loving commitment which travels as far as possible along the road of scientific knowledge and then takes its leap into the unprovable *in the direction of the trend of the evidence,* depending on the trustworthiness of God's nature and character as Christ revealed him.

Chapter 10

If I don't get better, is God's plan defeated?

THE ANSWER TO THIS QUESTION MUST BE A TRIUMPHANT "NO!" A God who could be ultimately defeated by factors which he had allowed to function in his universe would be no God at all. The very idea of omnipotence is not that everything that happens does so because God wills it in the sense of intending it. The truth about omnipotence is that nothing that does happen, even though it springs from man's misused free will, or from the human family's mass ignorance, or from folly or sin can *finally* defeat God. That is where omnipotence comes in.

If a sufferer reaches the point when he can no longer believe that he is going to recover in this life, even then I think he should try to co-operate with those who are doing their best to make him well. He need not regard his suffering even from the human standpoint as dead loss. His physicians may learn something by which they can help other sufferers, and who knows when a cure of his particular malady may be found?

At the same time, I feel I must write down my long-considered opinion that where a patient is in constant agony for which no relief can be found, and from which, humanly speaking, nothing can be learned, the quiet committing of the soul to God and the ending of physical life would not win from me censure of the doctor or criticism of the patient. Into this vexed and difficult question of euthanasia—or easy death, as it is called—I must not take the space to enter fully; but when one remembers how fortuitously, through the passion of parents, a life is sometimes begun, how ready a doctor is to destroy an infant life if the mother's is endangered; how men in millions have been led to death in war, or have been executed by the processes of the law or by tyrants like Hitler; how bravely, thinking of others, men like Captain Oates have gone to their deaths, and how determined men are to punish those who make an animal linger in long-continued pain, I see no reason in logic or religion why a patient for whom life has become unendurable and who can see no end to physical suffering, no value in it, no cowardly retreat from sharing responsibilities he ought not to evade, and only relief for those who look on, should not be allowed to slip away before the dignity of human nature is lowered any further. Were this made legal, all other outcomes having been discussed from a Christian and medical angle, I would myself give such a patient Holy Communion and stay with him while the doctor, whose responsibility I should thus share, did what was necessary to help one life to end and another begin. As yet it is not legal—though it is widely practiced—and we must keep the law.

This being so, the Christian attitude to continued suffering must be acceptance and co-operation. These are the words which seem to me the best to describe man's ideal attitude to the suffering which he cannot remedy.

Acceptance of a share, still more the willing acceptance of more than our full share, in the tragedy of life—a tragedy in which God, as well as man, is an actor—is positive; it has about it something vitalizing. . . . Those who meet pain clear-eyed, and with a positive and active acceptance, who "face the music" as the slang phrase has it; those who are not only ready to do their bit, but to share their bit in the world's sorrow, make a great discovery. They find not only that they are enabled to bear their sorrow in a way which hurts less—for that which hurts most in the bearing is that which is most resented; what is most freely accepted hurts least—but that they achieve an enrichment and a growth in personality which makes them centers of influence and light in ways of which they never suspected the possibility. Few things can so inspire and re-create the human heart as the spectacle of crushing misfortune cheerfully and heroically borne; and the unconscious influence which those exert is far greater than they or others comprehend. Suffering lightly borne is constructive work . . . for pain conquered is power.[1]

Such acceptance takes a man right into the secret places of God's purposes, and into a fellowship which includes some of the finest souls who have ever breathed. And while we assert that suffering is not the will of God, it can never be too emphatically stated that there is an opportunity in suffering which it is God's will we should take and turn to our own, and the world's, highest advantage. A thousand things which are not the will of God will happen to us in a world arranged as this is, but nothing can happen to us which cannot be captured for God by taking the right attitude. There is an alchemy which turns all things into spiritual gold, and that alchemy is the right attitude to them. Ultimately, what happens to us does not matter. But our reaction to what happens to us matters greatly.

The experiences of pain will come to us all. But nothing can ever come to us that may not be captured for God and for the gain of our personal character by an adoption of the right attitude. To one man a set of experiences are great mysteries, baffling problems, heavy burdens. To another those selfsame experiences will be, in Samuel Rutherford's phrase, the kind of burden

[1] Lily Dougall, *God's Way with Man* (London: Student Christian Movement Press, 1924).

that "sails are to a ship, that wings are to a bird." What are to Martin Chuzzlewit desolating blows of fate are to Mark Tapley opportunities "for coming out strong." To one man, life's experiences are those of dark valleys, steep mountains, rough places. To another every valley becomes exalted, every mountain and hill is brought low, the rough places are made plain, because he has found an attitude which, applied to them, subdues them.

There are still many questions that we cannot answer about pain. Why could not God have brought about the same ends by a different means, cutting out the possibility of pain? There is no answer except to say that to all Wisdom the way he took was the best way. We may ask why God ever made a body and mind capable of feeling such pain; and if some answer that only such a being as man could climb, as man does, till his stride takes in the very stars, then others will say the price paid is too high. We have no faculty for a complete answer, but the lines of thought we have pursued in their cumulative strength seem to us to go as far as one need go. For the rest we may take as a parable an incident from Egypt.

When the Nile spread its obliterating deposit of black mud over fields hardly won from the desert, and watered at great cost of patient toil, the victor over it was not the engineer stemming its current with his barricade, but the inspired peasant who, greatly daring, flung his precious rice into the forbidding ooze, and waited for God to send the rich harvest.[2]

That is acceptance and co-operation. Where we cannot fight and overcome suffering, we are to take such an attitude to it that by co-operation with God we may bring a great harvest which

[2] John Oman, *Grace and Personality* (London: Cambridge University Press, 1919), p. 10.

shall enrich the spiritual wealth of the world and make glad the heart of God.

If even the heart is not satisfied, it will find its anchorage on that fundamental with which we began—the goodness of God. And it will find its final argument, not in the brain, but in those reasons which the heart alone can give.

> Yet, in the maddening maze of things,
>   And tossed by storm and flood,
> To one fixed trust my spirit clings;
>   I know that God is good!

"I KNOW." The world's thinking sufferers, from Job to Browning, have all said that triumphant word: "I know that my redeemer liveth"; "I know in whom I have believed."

> Sorrow is hard to bear and doubt is slow to clear;
>   Each sufferer has his say, his scheme of the weal and woe.
> But God has a few of us whom He whispers in the ear,
>   The rest may reason and welcome; 'tis we musicians *know*.

We cannot understand pain altogether, nor justify it, nor explain it, but we know him. That assurance runs like a silver cord through all the maze of men's experience through all the ages as they are confronted by this mystery. Better men than ourselves have found that just to hold to that cord and trust in the dark is in itself the defeat of pain. Though there should be every reason in the world to prove that God is a devil; that evil is more powerful than good; that there is no order, no purpose, no living design, no meaning in life at all, yet in the face of all argument to say, "I know," that is to keep alive the undying fire of faith and to

91

make of the very things that would quench it, fuel that shall make it a blazing furnace.

Thus we may not solve the mystery entirely, but we may rise above it, rob it of its power to quell us; more than that, we may turn its fruit of doubt into faith, its depression into victory, its evil into a power for good that none can stay, knowing if "God were one whit less than He is, He dare not put us into a world that carries so many arguments against Him." [3]

I should like to end the book by looking again at Jesus, the beloved Son who only sought to do his Father's will. How justifiably he might have asked the questions which stand at the head of some of the foregoing chapters! Did God know? Why should this happen to me? Where do God's goodness and omnipotence come in? What sense is there in it all? If I am killed, will God's plan be defeated?

I cannot myself avoid the conclusion that the Cross was no more the will of God than any other brutal murder. It was the work of wicked men, as Peter said on the day of Pentecost. Wicked men do not do the will of God. And I think the awful agony in the Garden of Gethsemane was our Lord's dread lest God's plan should be defeated. He had hoped to convince the multitudes himself. When that looked like failing he hoped the twelve would carry the good news through the land. And what good news it was! God was the loving Father of all, and all were brothers. All men of all nations were dear to him and all could bring from the North and the South and the East and the West their treasures of mind and heart and make one world kingdom with no nation but humanity and with no king but God.

Then he had been betrayed, deserted, arrested, and the Cross

---

[3] Letters to his friends for private circulation by Forbes Robinson.

looked like, and felt like, and was called the end. As that Cross loomed up, no wonder that he who had said so confidently, "With God all things are possible," cried out, *"If it be possible,* let this cup pass." (Matt. 19:26; 26:39.)

For some sufferer who reads this book something similar may have happened. A young mother faces death and wonders, as Christ did, however the purposes of God can possibly be worked out. She may be leaving young children. A young man is taken, as Christ was, at the height of his powers. A young father, the breadwinner, dies, leaving a little family behind. . . .

Yet still those things that God did not plan or intend can be woven into a pattern which serves his purposes and which none can destroy. The Cross has meant that far more spiritual power has been released into the world than if Jesus had lived to a ripe old age and died in quiet retirement. And God can weave our lesser sorrows and sufferings into a plan which will leave us with no sense of loss at last. God can flash to us code messages by means of lamps which he did not light. Jesus might have said to Caiaphas and those who plotted his death what Joseph said to his brethren, "You meant evil against me; but God meant it for good" (Gen. 50:20). And those whose sorrows have been brought upon them by evil men will one day say the same.

Even death itself, I think, matters hardly at all if only we can glimpse the perspective of God's age-long plan. Whether I continue to live and work on this plane or on the next, on this side of death or on the other, probably makes no more difference to God's purposes than whether I live in Manchester or Leeds.

For life goes on. I am as sure of that as of any tenet in the Christian creed. I feel I want to say to anyone suffering from what is called incurable diesease: "Only the body dies. To answer the question at the head of this chapter, you *will* get better. You will wake up on a spiritual plane of love and activity and service and eternal youth, unhampered by pain and disease and the limitations of old age, creaky muscles, hardened arteries, and laboring breath; and you will find that you have only parted with a worn-out overcoat called the body. The real 'you' is immortal, and you will greet your dear ones again and go on spiritually where you left off here."

No one at death has exhausted his possibilities. Some at death have hardly begun to live. If death meant annihilation, then nature would be as irrational as would be the death of every bird before it left its shell. Within that imprisoning shell are wings and a throat and the structure of eyes. One day, when the shell is broken, they will function. The difference will be that of the huddled body, cramped up in a shell, and a skylark on poised wing in the sunlit air pouring out its song in the glory of a new life. We too shall enter a new phase of activity and realized possibility.

So, dear sufferer, I salute you, knowing that no words of mine can ease your pain, hoping only that in a world in which none of us can see very far, a thought here and there may ease a bewildered mind or a troubled spirit, "to give light to them that sit in darkness and in the shadow of death; and to guide our feet into the way of peace."

A Prayer

O GOD, WHO DWELLEST IN UNAPPROACHABLE MYSTERY AND whose ways are far beyond our understanding, help us to rest our minds in the certainty that we are dear to thee in spite of all our weaknesses and failures. Forgive us if, sometimes, suffering fills all our horizon and we find no comfort in any word of man or any thought of thee. Draw very near to us in the tenderness and compassion which overflowed from thee into the heart of Christ, and, for his sake, keep alive the flickering flame of our faith and hope and love. Show us the pathway of thy will for us in each day and in each circumstance. If it may be, lighten our burden, gladden our eyes, comfort our hearts, heal the sick body, and quiet the troubled mind. But whatever may lie ahead, give us the assurance that thy friendliness enwraps us, that a wondrous purpose that cannot be defeated is being worked out in our lives, and that nothing can ever snatch us from thy loving care. So at last, without regret and without dishonor, bring us to our journey's end in peace. AMEN.